AF372988

Illustrations and Text by Skadi Cooke

ISBN 9798988606307

Vulture and Crone
Harper's Ferry, West Virginia
publishing.vultureandcrone@gmail.com

For Cal

LET'S TALK WITH PICTURES

by Skadi Cooke

I talk in pictures.

Would you like to see?

Look! These cards

all make words for me.

This one means

I'm happy.

This one means I'm sad. 

This one

means I'm hungry.

Yuck! This tastes bad.

 This one means too noisy.

This means

I want to play. 

HAPPY
CAR
FAVORITE COLOR

I might be kind of quiet, but I have a lot to say!

**Some kids
use their mouths to talk.**

Others use their hands.

But I use cards to talk, and

now you can understand!

ABOUT THE AUTHOR

Skadi Cooke lives with their very silly family on the side of a mountain in West Virginia. They love frogs, having ice cream for breakfast and the color blue. They really hope you like this book.